PHOENIX HINKLEY

Phoenix Hinkley was born somewhere in the woods in England shortly after a major UFO sighting in the 70s. He started his working career in the media industry working as a producer and writer for a TV and video production company in Manchester. The advert with the talking animals at Knowsley Safari Park – that was his.

Since then he's been a machine operator, a baker, a hearing aid technician, a pot washer and a price controller. He fully acknowledges that his CV is a little bit weird.

He has written a bunch of other books under a different name. Don't look for them, they're not there anymore. Well, they are but he refuses to disclose any further information on the matter.

He lives in Warrington, England – also in the Birthplace of Tim Curry!

www.facebook.com/phoenixhinkley
www.twitter.com/phoenixhinkley
www.instagram.com/phoenixhinkley

Also by Killian H. Gore

Before Halloween
The Thingy From Another World
Beyond Bigfoot
The Demon of Heritage
Three Tales of Terror
The Horror Movie Massacre: Books One & Two
The Exorcist Steps
UFO of the Dead

Non-fiction:

The Unauthorized Friday the 13th Quiz Book
The 'Burbs Unauthorized Quiz Book
Incredible Horror Movie Facts 1&2
The Evil Dead Unauthorized Quiz Book
What's Your Favorite Scary Movie?
Phantasm Unauthorized Quiz Book
The Thing Unauthorized Quiz Book
Jaws Unauthorized Quiz Book
The Monster Squad Unauthorized Quiz Book
The Shining Unauthorized Quiz Book
The Huge Horror Movie Quiz Book
Gremlins Unauthorized Quiz Book
Plan 9 from Outer Space Quiz Book
Horror Movie Crossword Book 1&2
Halloween Unauthorized Quiz Book
The Horror Movie Manual
Serial Killer Quiz Book
Horror Movie Word Search Quiz Book
UFO Quiz Book
The Demented World of Dustin Ferguson
The Real Friday the 13th
The Horror Movie Labyrinth
Horror Flix Pix: Horror Picture Puzzles
The Huge Slasher Movie Quiz Book
The Burning Unauthorized Quiz Book
An American Werewolf in London Unauthorized Quiz Book

—

ABOUT THE AUTHORS

KILLIAN H. GORE

Killian H. Gore was born in Fort Phantom in Texas in 1976. He is a distant relative of the serial killer Ellen Mort who was born in Liverpool, England and later vanished in Salt Lake City, Utah, after violently butchering all five of her husbands (*for the full true story of Ellen Mort, read my Incredible Horror Movie Facts book*).

He is the author of the short story collections *Before Halloween* and *Three Tales of Terror* as well as the novellas *Beyond Bigfoot, The Thingy From Another World, The Demon of Heritage, UFO of the Dead* and the serialized horror story, *The Horror Movie Massacre.*

His short films *Schrecken, Two Ghost Tent* and *Don't Look at the Camera!* appear in the *60 Seconds to Die* horror film series. He is also an Associate Producer of the 2021 summer camp slasher movie, *Bloody Summer Camp*, starring Felissa Rose.

His hugely entertaining *What's Your Favorite Scary Movie?* book features interviews with such horror legends as Joe Dante, Michael Berryman, Richard Stanley, John A. Russo, Marcus Nispel, Fred Dekker, William Malone, and Mark Shostrom. He's also written a whole bunch of quiz books! Listen out for Killian on *The Huge Horror Movie Podcast* on YouTube

He lives in Warrington, England – The Birthplace of Tim Curry!

www.facebook.com/killianhgore
www.twitter.com/killianhgore
www.instagram/killianhgore
For SIGNED COPIES and HORROR HAMPERS (including The Rocky Horror Lovers Hamper!) check out the Killian Gore Store on Etsy

The Lost Boys Unauthorized Quiz Book
Pet Sematary Unauthorized Quiz Book
Creepshow Unauthorized Quiz Book
Black Christmas Unauthorized Quiz Book
House Unauthorized Quiz Book
Creature from the Black Lagoon Unauthorized Quiz Book
Shaun of the Dead Unauthorized Quiz Book
Sleepaway Camp Unauthorized Quiz Book
Behind the Mask Unauthorized Quiz Book
Troll 2 Unauthorized Quiz Book
The Return of the Living Dead Unauthorized Quiz Book
Psycho Unauthorized Quiz Book
Fright Night Unauthorized Quiz Book
The Blair Witch Project Unauthorized Quiz Book
Scream Unauthorized Quiz Book
The Exorcist Unauthorized Quiz Book
Cannibal Holocaust Unauthorized Quiz Book
The Silence of the Lambs Unauthorized Quiz Book
Salem's Lot Unauthorized Quiz Book
Killer Klowns from Outer Space Unauthorized Quiz Book
Candyman Unauthorized Quiz Book
Session 9 Unauthorized Quiz Book
Night of the Living Dead Unauthorized Quiz Book
Dawn of the Dead Unauthorized Quiz Book

Also by Phoenix Hinkley

This Is Spinal Tap Unauthorized Quiz Book
National Lampoon's Vacation Unauthorized Quiz Book
The Princess Bride Unauthorized Quiz Book
The Wizard of Oz Unauthorized Quiz Book
Groundhog Day Unauthorized Quiz Book
Scrooged Unauthorized Quiz Book

Also by Killian H. Gore and Phoenix Hinkley

The League of Gentlemen Unauthorised Quiz Book
Garth Marenghi's Darkplace Unauthorised Quiz Book

—

—

THE ROCKY HORROR PICTURE SHOW

Unauthorised QUIZ BOOK

By
Killian H. Gore and Phoenix Hinkley

Contents

The Rocky Horror Picture Show – Questions...............11
The Rocky Horror Picture Show – Answers.................51
Double Difficult Rocky Horror – Questions................61
Double Difficult Rocky Horror – Answers..................71
Shock Treatment – Questions................................77
Shock Treatment – Answers.................................85
The Rocky Horror Picture Show Filming Locations.........89
A Strange Journey (short story by Killian H. Gore
and Phoenix Hinkley)..101
Transylvanian Guests..115

THE ROCKY HORROR PICTURE SHOW

Questions

1. **Before a last-minute title change to *The Rocky Horror Show*, what was the working title of the original 1973 stage show?**

A) Rocky Horror Shows His Heels
B) The Brad and Janet Show
C) They Came from Denton High
D) Revenge of the Old Queen

2. **Whose lips are on the screen for the opening song, *Science Fiction/Double Feature*?**

A) Richard O'Brien's
B) Tim Curry's
C) Patricia Quinn's
D) Little Nell's

3. **In the stage version *of The Rocky Horror Show*, what is the name of the character who sings *Science Fiction/Double Feature*?**

A) The Projectionist
B) The Usherette
C) The Conductor
D) The Impresario

4. **What is NOT one of the classic sci-fi movies mentioned in the lyrics of *Science Fiction/Double Feature*?**

A) Tarantula
B) When Worlds Collide
C) It Came from Outer Space
D) War of the Worlds

5. At which church does the marriage of Brad and Janet's friends, Ralph and Betty Hapschatt, take place at the beginning of the movie?

A) Denton Fundamentalist Church
B) Denton Episcopalian Church
C) Denton Presbyterian Church
D) Denton Transylvanian Church

6. Aside from the actress playing Magenta often playing a dual role, which other characters are often performed by the same actor in live shows?

A) Eddie and The Narrator
B) Eddie and Riff Raff
C) Eddie and Dr. Scott
D) Eddie and Frank-N-Furter

7. Finish the words that are written in shaving foam on the side of Ralph and Betty's wedding car: Wait Til Tonite... ?

A) She Got Hers Now He'll Get His
B) He's Hot His Now She'll Get Hers
C) She Said I Do Now I'm Doing
D) Smiling Will Make Her Face Ache

8. Richard O'Brien's American Gothic character outside the church is holding something throughout the wedding scene – what is it?

A) A scythe
B) A pitchfork
C) A shovel
D) A hoe

9. Who from the original 1973 cast of *The Rocky Horror Show* did not play the same character in the feature film?

A) Richard O'Brien
B) Nell Campbell
C) Jonathan Adams
D) Patricia Quinn

10. Outside the church there is a sign that is clearly visible, what do the words on it say?

A) His Path Within For Those Without
B) Be True To Every Inmost Thought
C) Presume Thou Not To Teach
D) Be Just And Fear Not

11. How long does Brad say that Ralph will be in line for a promotion?

A) One year
B) A year or two
C) Two or three years
D) A few months

12. Which popular comedic actor was said to have auditioned for the role of Brad Majors in *The Rocky Horror Picture Show*?

A) Rock Moranis
B) Martin Short
C) Steve Martin
D) Robin Williams

13. What is the missing word from the Denton sign: Denton The _____ of Happiness?

A) Land
B) Town
C) Home
D) Place

14. What is the tagline on the 1975 theatrical release poster for *The Rocky Horror Picture Show*?

A) One From The Vault!
B) The Music Made Him Do It!
C) It's Not Just A Movie… It's An Event!
D) He's The Hero – That's Right, The Hero!!

15. As Brad sings *Damn It, Janet*, what does he dash over to draw in chalk on the church doors?

A) A heart
B) A wedding ring
C) A kiss (lips)
D) The letters B and J

16. The filmmakers wanted the beginning of the film to be different to how it turned out in the final cut – how did they originally want the movie to start?

A) With no spoken dialogue – just all singing
B) Shown in black and white
C) Have it be framed by theatre curtains
D) Have it be in mono

17. When listing the three ways that love can grow in *Damn It, Janet*, what is the third way?

A) Middling

B) Moderate
C) Medium
D) Mediocre

18. Which iconic music artist did Meat Loaf say came to watch *The Rocky Horror Show* during its run at the Roxy Theatre in Los Angeles in 1974?

A) Frank Sinatra
B) David Bowie
C) Elvis Presley
D) John Lennon

19. Whilst Brad and Janet sing inside the church, what do the American Gothic family carry in through the vestry door?

A) A large crucifix
B) A coffin
C) A bouquet of flowers
D) A box of bibles

20. Who is the music composer that worked with Richard O'Brien on the score arrangement and incidental music for *The Rocky Horror Picture Show*?

A) Doug Besterman
B) Kris Kukul
C) Paul Lavender
D) Richard Hartley

21. In which month does The Criminologist say that Brad and Janet left Denton to visit Doctor Everett Scott?

A) April
B) July

C) September
D) November

22. Who was the only performer from the original London cast of *The Rocky Horror Show* that starred in the 1974 Roxy Theatre production of the show?

A) Richard O'Brien
B) Little Nell
C) Tim Curry
D) Patricia Quinn

23. What is the title of the large leatherbound book that The Criminologist flips through when he's introducing the story?

A) The Denton Dossier
B) The Denton Affair
C) The Denton Case
D) The Denton File

24. What is usually shouted out at the screen by the audience when The Criminologist first talks about Brad and Janet?

A) Jerk for Brad, Whore for Janet
B) Asshole for Brad, Slut for Janet
C) Dickhead for Brad, Bimbo for Janet
D) Prick for Brad, Tart for Janet

25. As Brad and Janet drive through the rain, what is Janet eating in the car?

A) A banana
B) An apple
C) A chocolate bar
D) Popcorn

26. How many motorcyclists does Janet observe have passed them whilst they have been driving?

A) Two
B) Three
C) Four
D) Five

27. What are live screenings of *The Rocky Horror Picture Show* called where the film is screened behind a group of performers recreating the film for the audience?

A) Showcasts
B) Shadowplays
C) Pictureplays
D) Shadowcasts

28. A famous news story plays over the radio when Brad and Janet are driving – what is it?

A) President Nixon's resignation
B) The Apollo 11 Moon landing
C) The JFK assassination
D) Martin Luther King's "I Have a Dream" speech

29. Which cast member from *The Rocky Horror Picture Show* was once thrown out of a screening of the movie for being an imposter?

A) Meat Loaf
B) Tim Curry
C) Richard O'Brien
D) Little Nell

30. What is written on the sign hanging on the front gates of the castle?

A) Danger Of Death
B) Violators Will Be Shot
C) Enter At Your Own Risk!!
D) Private Keep Out

31. Finish Janet's lyric from the beginning of *Over at the Frankenstein Place*:

In the velvet darkness of the... ?

A) Deepest night
B) Burning night
C) Starkest night
D) Blackest night

32. What do audience members watching *Rocky Horror* hold over their heads when *Over at the Frankenstein Place* is performed?

A) Umbrellas
B) Frankenstein masks
C) Newspapers
D) Inflatable stars

33. When Riff Raff first appears to sing his part in *Over at the Frankenstein Place*, where is he?

A) In the front doorway
B) In an upstairs window
C) On the roof of the castle
D) Sitting on a motorcycle

34. What is the name of the mansion house in Windsor that was used for Dr. Frank N. Furter's castle in the movie?

A) Ettington Park
B) Knebworth House
C) Oakley Court
D) Culzean Castle

35. Which word does Riff Raff use when he opens the front door of the castle to Brad and Janet?

A) Yes?
B) Hello
C) Welcome
D) Evening

36. Which popular game show did Richard O'Brien go on to host in 1990?

A) Treasure Hunt
B) Gladiators
C) The Crystal Maze
D) Fort Boyard

37. Speculating that the castle could be some kind of hunting lodge, who does Brad think it could be for?

A) Rich freaks
B) Rich screwballs
C) Rich crackpots
D) Rich weirdos

38. When the US stage production of *The Rocky Horror Show* moved from the Roxy Theatre over to the Belasco Theatre on Broadway, the main cast were the same, but which performer from the original London cast replaced one of the Roxy roles?

A) Christopher Malcolm
B) Richard O'Brien
C) Julie Covington
D) Jonathan Adams

39. When Magenta reveals herself on the staircase in front of Riff Raff, Brad, and Janet, what does she throw to Riff Raff?

A) A feather duster
B) A pair of rubber gloves
C) A mop
D) A loofah

40. At the beginning of *The Time Warp*, what is the time on the coffin clock?

A) 9 o'clock
B) 10 o'clock
C) 11 o'clock
D) 12 o'clock

41. Which statement is true about the coffin clock that was used in the movie?

A) It belonged to Vincent Price
B) It also appeared in The House in Nightmare Park (1973)
C) It contained a real skeleton
D) It was stolen during the making of the movie

42. What really drives you insane in *The Time Warp*?

A) The perfect thrust
B) The pelvic thrust
C) The pellet thrust
D) The penis thrust

43. Which famous painting is visible above all the fireplaces in the ballroom as *The Time Warp* is being performed?

A) The Last Supper
B) Mona Lisa
C) The Scream
D) Whistler's Mother

44. Which rock group released a cover of *The Time Warp* in 2020 in support of the Rock the Vote presidential campaign in the US?

A) Spinal Tap
B) The Darkness
C) Tenacious D
D) Steel Panther

45. First seen during *The Time Warp*, which well-known British actor and TV presenter appears as one of the Transylvanians?

A) Lionel Blair
B) Christopher Biggins
C) Timmy Mallett
D) Derek Griffiths

46. After *The Time Warp* has finished, which dance does Brad ask the Transylvanians if they know how to do?

A) The Monkey
B) The Mashed Potato
C) The Monster Mash
D) The Madison

47. When singing *Sweet Transvestite*, which lyric does Dr. Frank-N-Furter sing just before whipping off his cape?

A) He thought you were the candy man
B) Don't get strung out by the way I look
C) But by night I'm one hell of a lover
D) Don't judge a book by its cover

48. What does the writing above Frank-N-Furter's heart tattoo on his right shoulder say?

A) BOSS
B) LOVE
C) HOT DOG
D) SWEET

49. As well as taking inspiration from his own mother, who else has Tim Curry said influenced how Frank-N-Furter speaks and acts?

A) Joanna Lumley
B) Hattie Jacques
C) Barbara Woodhouse
D) Queen Elizabeth II

**50. What does Frank-N-Further throw directly into the
camera whilst singing *Sweet Transvestite*?**

A) Wine
B) Confetti
C) Water
D) Beer

**51. How many seconds is the pause between "antici"
and "pation" in *Sweet Transvestite*?**

A) 1 seconds
B) 2 seconds
C) 3 seconds
D) 4 seconds

**52. Which actor has NOT starred as Frank-N-Furter in
one of the stage productions of *The Rocky Horror Show*?**

A) Jonathan Wilkes
B) David Arquette
C) Duncan James
D) Adrian Edmondson

**53. Before Riff Raff closes the elevator doors on the way
up to the laboratory, what does he drop onto the floor?**

A) Brad and Janet's clothes
B) A Champagne bottle
C) A wine glass
D) A cup of water

**54. When introducing himself and Janet to Frank, what
does Brad accidentally give Janet's surname as?**

A) Rice
B) Nice

C) Vice
D) Spice

**55. Clearly a fan, Rob Zombie featured characters in
Rocky Horror outfits in *Halloween II* (2009) and then
went one step further by casting Patricia Quinn in
which of his movies?**

A) The Munsters
B) 31
C) 3 from Hell
D) The Lords of Salem

**56. When addressing his "unconventional
conventionalists," what does Frank tell them they're
about to witness a new breakthrough in?**

A) Biosphere research
B) Biochemical research
C) Biotech research
D) Biodegradation research

57. What colour are Frank's rubber gloves?

A) Pink
B) Red
C) Blue
D) Yellow

**58. Which legendary rock star was said to have been
interested in playing the role of Frank-N-Furter in the
movie?**

A) Freddie Mercury
B) Roger Daltrey
C) Mick Jagger
D) David Bowie

59. How many more points does Frank tell Riff Raff to step up the reactor power input by?

A) Two more
B) Three more
C) Four more
D) Five more

60. Bray Studios, where some of *The Rocky Horror Picture Show* was filmed, was heavily associated with which British movies?

A) The Hammer Films
B) The Carry On Films
C) The Ealing Studios Films
D) The James Bond Films

61. When Frank first sees Rocky's face, what does he say?

A) Oh baby!
B) Hoopla!
C) Oh my!
D) Oh Rocky!

62. Which horror movie had the tank where Rocky is created originally been used in?

A) Dracula Has Risen from the Grave
B) The Mummy's Shroud
C) The Revenge of Frankenstein
D) The Curse of the Werewolf

63. Which is the correct spelling of the title of the song that Rocky sings after coming to life?

A) The Sword of Damoclies

B) The Sword of Damocles
C) The Sword of Damachlies
D) The Sword of Damaclees

64. What is the character of Rocky Horror missing from his body?

A) Nipples
B) A belly button
C) Fingernails
D) An Adam's apple

65. What is Columbia's lacklustre opinion of Rocky after Riff Raff says he's a credit to Frank's genius?

A) He's alright
B) He's not bad
C) He's pretty good
D) He's okay

66. Which song from *The Rocky Horror Picture Show* is presented in a much shorter version in the US theatrical version of the movie?

A) I'm Going Home
B) Wild and Untamed Thing
C) Superheroes
D) Rose Tint My World

67. Whose seal of approval does Frank say Rocky carries, after Janet says she doesn't like men with too many muscles?

A) Charles Atlas'
B) Steve Reeves'
C) Johnny Weissmuller's
D) Reg Park's

68. In the opening credits to *The Rocky Horror Picture Show*, each main character is given a description in brackets – what does it say for Peter Hinwood's Rocky Horror character?

A) A Muscle Man
B) A Creation
C) A Monster
D) A Creature

69. What is the last word of the lyric in *I Can Make You a Man*:

Do the snatch, clean, and…

A) Perk
B) Smerk
C) Zerk
D) Jerk

70. In which other popular movie does Tim Curry play a character in a large mansion house as other characters come in from the rain, one of whom wants to use the phone?

A) Haunted Honeymoon
B) Clue
C) High Spirits
D) Bloodbath at the House of Death

71. What is written upon the back of Eddie's leather jacket?

A) EDDIE
B) LOVE
C) BABY
D) HATE

72. On which American comedy show did Tim Curry and Meat Loaf appear in a sketch about a Rocky Horror Shop?

A) The Tracey Ullman Show
B) SCTV
C) The Muppet Show
D) Saturday Night Live

73. Which popular music star plays the role of Eddie in the 2016 remake, *The Rocky Horror Picture Show: Let's Do the Time Warp Again*?

A) Adam Lambert
B) Chris Daughtry
C) David Cook
D) Phillip Phillips

74. Which musical instrument does Eddie start to play in the middle of *Hot Patootie – Bless My Soul*?

A) A trumpet
B) A saxophone
C) A harmonica
D) A piano

75. In the 1980s, which future Hollywood star played Eddie in both Australian and New Zealand productions of *The Rocky Horror Show*?

A) Sam Neill
B) Huge Jackman
C) Guy Pearce
D) Russell Crowe

**76. At the end of Eddie's *Hot Patootie – Bless My Soul*
song, what does Frank kill him with?**

A) An axe
B) A meat cleaver
C) An ice pick
D) A chainsaw

**77. What is NOT one of the things commonly thrown at
live shows and screenings of *Rocky Horror*?**

A) Rice
B) Rose petals
C) Toilet paper
D) Toast

**78. In the *I Can Make You a Man (Reprise)*, which lyric
does Janet interrupt Frank to sing?**

A) Dig it, if you can
B) Just dynamic tension
C) A hot groin and a tricep
D) I'm a muscle fan

**79. Which legendary horror star was initially sought for
the role of The Criminologist?**

A) Vincent Price
B) Peter Cushing
C) Christopher Lee
D) Donald Pleasence

80. What is the second part of The Criminologists line?

"There are some people who say that life is an illusion, and that reality is…"

A) Just a big stage show
B) Simply a figment of the imagination
C) Much weirder than anyone's imagination
D) A dream within a dream

81. Two big Hollywood stars appeared as The Criminologist/Narrator in the 35th Anniversary benefit performance of *The Rocky Horror Show* – who were they?

A) Bill Murray and Dan Aykroyd
B) Tom Cruise and Ben Stiller
C) Robert DeNiro and Al Pacino
D) Jack Nicholson and Danny DeVito

82. When Frank sneaks into Janet's bedroom pretending to be Brad, how does she first become aware that he's not really Brad?

A) She pulls his glasses off
B) She sees his tattoos
C) She pulls his wig off
D) She feels his stiletto heels

83. Who recorded the commentary track for *The Rocky Horror Picture Show*, which has appeared on DVD and Blu-ray releases of the movie?

A) Tim Curry and Richard O'Brien
B) Richard O' Brien and Patricia Quinn
C) Patricia Quinn and Little Nell
D) Susan Sarandon and Barry Bostwick

84. What is Magenta doing just before Riff Raff goes to torment Rocky in the bridal chamber?

A) Dusting the control panel
B) Hoovering the floor
C) Polishing a statue
D) Mopping the floor

85. When tormenting Rocky in the bridal chamber, what does Riff Raff keep shoving toward him?

A) A mop
B) A candelabra
C) A pitchfork
D) A ray gun

86. Which of the following behind the scenes trivia is NOT true about the making of *The Rocky Horror Picture Show*?

A) Some of the actors weren't told Eddie's body was under the dinner table
B) Both Meat Loaf and his stunt performer were injured shooting the motorcycle scenes
C) One of the Transylvania extras had previously appeared in The Wizard of Oz (1939)
D) The scene with Dr. Scott crashing through the lab wall was improvised because the crew forgot to build a door on the set

87. In promising not to tell Janet about him and Brad in bed together, what does Frank swear on?

A) His mother's grave
B) His father's grave
C) His grandmother's grave
D) His grandfather's grave

88. Who directed *The Rocky Horror Picture Show* – and the original stage show?

A) Trey Parker
B) Frank Oz
C) Darren Lynn Bousman
D) Jim Sharman

89. When Janet takes the elevator up to the laboratory, she begins listing various "if only" statements – what is NOT one of them?

A) If only the car hadn't broken down
B) If only Dr. Scott was with us
C) If only we were amongst friends or sane persons
D) If only we hadn't made this journey

90. The original 1975 release of the soundtrack to *The Rocky Horror Picture Show* omitted two songs from the film – what were they?

A) I Can Make You a Man and Hot Patootie – Bless My Soul
B) Eddie and Rose Tint My World
C) I'm Going Home and Dammit Janet
D) The Sword of Damocles and Planet, Schmanet, Janet

91. Where does Janet get a piece of material from to dress Rocky's wound?

A) From her petticoat
B) From Rocky's discarded bandages
C) From the red sheet Rocky was hiding under
D) From an old towel

92. Throughout *Touch-a, Touch-a, Touch-a, Touch Me*, what is Magenta doing?

A) Applying lip gloss
B) Using a hair dryer
C) Buffing her nails
D) Brushing her hair

93. In which Ben Stiller and Owen Wilson movie does Susan Sarandon make an uncredited appearance, saying her Janet line, "Touch-a, touch-a, touch-a, touch me, I want to be dirty"?

A) Zoolander 2
B) Meet the Parents
C) Starsky & Hutch
D) Night at the Museum

94. In *Touch-a, Touch-a, Touch-a, Touch Me*, what are the two separate words that Columbia and Magenta both repeat together from the lyrics?

A) Know and Go
B) Getting and Petting
C) More and Down
D) Hand and Action

95. Throughout the movie there are various references to something in the movie world, for example The Criminologist's globe, the gong used to announce the serving of dinner, and Columbia's mouse ears – what do all these things represent?

A) Musical stars
B) Alien movies
C) B movie directors
D) Film studios

**96. When each character takes a turn singing the lyric
"Creature of the night," in *Touch-a, Touch-a, Touch-a,
Touch Me*, who is the last person to sing before Janet
ends the song?**

A) Columbia
B) Rocky
C) Frank
D) Riff Raff

**97. Which song from the original production of *The
Rocky Horror Show* was filmed but omitted from the
final cut of the movie?**

A) Once in a While
B) Love at First Sight
C) No Hiding Place
D) Little Old Heart Stopping Me

**98. What does Riff Raff slipup by saying when Brad
recognises Dr. Everett Scott on the monitor?**

A) You know this human?
B) You know this mortal?
C) You know this humanoid?
D) You know this earthling?

**99. Which movie, which had its premiere at the
International Rocky Horror Fan Convention in 2001,
starred Richard O'Brien as Lord Vladimere Hellsubus?**

A) Love Bites
B) Thir13en Ghosts
C) Elvira's Haunted Hills
D) The Happiness of the Katakuris

100. Which branch of the Bureau of Investigation does Frank state to Brad that he knows Dr. Scott works for?

A) Aliens
B) UFOs
C) Extra-terrestrials
D) Flying saucers

101. Whilst in the Zen Room, what does Dr. Scott pick up and look at under a magnifying glass?

A) A cigarette butt
B) A pen
C) A tube of lipstick
D) A fork

102. Jonathan Adams (Dr. Scott) was in the original 1973 theatre production of *The Rocky Horror Show*, but in a different role than in the film adaptation – which character was he in the stage show?

A) Rocky Horror
B) Brad Majors
C) Narrator
D) Eddie

103. What is the name of the electronic magnet that Frank uses to bring Dr. Scott up to the lab with?

A) Single Contact Electro Magnet
B) Double Contact Electro Magnet
C) Triple Contact Electro Magnet
D) Quadruple Contact Electro Magnet

**104. In the, *"Janet! Dr. Scott! Janet! Brad! Rocky!"*
exchange, how many times does Frank say "Rocky"?**

A) Two times
B) Three times
C) Four times
D) Five times

**105. Having created the iconic character of Frank-N-
Furter, Tim Curry went on to create another iconic
character in 1990 – who was it?**

A) Pinhead
B) Hannibal Lector
C) Pennywise
D) Ghostface

**106. Regarding the dinner that everyone is about to
have, what does The Criminologist say there will be
very little of amongst the guests?**

A) Rapport
B) Bonhomie
C) Cordiality
D) Camaraderie

**107. What are newcomers to attending *Rocky Horror*
stage show and film screenings known as?**

A) Rookies
B) Newbies
C) Virgins
D) Freshmen

108. Whilst slicing the meat, what causes Frank to menacingly point the electric meat carver at one of his guests?

A) Rocky picks up his glass of wine
B) Dr. Scott picks up his glass of wine
C) Brad picks up his glass of wine
D) Janet picks up her glass of wine

109. Which member of the Royal Family once told Tim Curry that they were a fan of *The Rocky Horror Picture Show*?

A) Prince Edward
B) Queen Elizabeth II
C) Prince William
D) Princess Diana

110. What does Frank liberally pour onto his dinner?

A) Mustard
B) Ketchup
C) Salt
D) Vinegar

111. In the song, *Eddie*, who sings the lyric, "He was a low down cheap little punk"?

A) The Criminologist
B) Frank-N-Furter
C) Dr. Scott
D) Riff Raff

112. *The Rocky Horror Picture Show* wasn't an immediate box office success – how did the movie eventually find its audience?

A) As a double feature with Shock Treatment
B) As a VHS home video release
C) As a Midnight Movie
D) As a Super 8 release, featuring selected scenes

113. What is the correct first line written on Eddie's note that his voice reads out during the *Eddie* song?

A) I'm out of my heyd
B) I'm out my hed
C) I'm out of my heed
D) I'm out of my had

114. Who was NOT one of the guest Narrators for the *Rocky Horror Show Live* (2015)?

A) Christopher Biggins
B) Stephen Fry
C) Emma Bunton
D) Mel Giedroyc

115. After Frank reveals Eddie's mutilated body, who is the first person to exit the dining room?

A) Frank
B) Dr. Scott
C) Brad
D) Janet

116. Which actor played Frank-N-Furter in the 2015 live recording of *The Rocky Horror Show* that was broadcast live to cinemas in the UK and Europe?

A) Anthony Head
B) David Bedella
C) Craig McLachlan
D) Stephen Webb

117. In the song *Planet Schmanet Janet*, what does Frank say Janet is as sensual as?

A) A pencil
B) Fennel
C) A kennel
D) A pretzel

118. In stage productions of *The Rocky Horror Show*, what are the minor background characters referred to as?

A) Transylvanians
B) Ghosts
C) Phantoms
D) Usherettes

119. What is the name of the audio-vibratory, physio-molecular transport device that Frank uses on Brad, Janet, and Dr. Scott to glue them to the spot?

A) Sonic Seducer
B) Sonic Reducer
C) Sonic Transducer
D) Sonic Inducer

120. What is the title of the short song that is performed as Brad, Janet, and Dr. Scott are turned into statues with the Medusa Machine?

A) Hot and Flustered
B) Planet Hot Dog
C) Don't Hurt Her, Frank Furter
D) You're a Hot Dog

121. Which two stars from *The Rocky Horror Picture Show* appeared in the 2010 *Glee* episode, *The Rocky Horror Glee Show*?

A) Richard O'Brien and Patricia Quinn
B) Susan Sarandon and Barry Bostwick
C) Meat Loaf and Barry Bostwick
D) Little Nell and Tim Curry

122. Who is the last character to be turned into a statue by the Medusa Machine?

A) Columbia
B) Dr. Scott
C) Janet
D) Rocky

123. The more iconic poster for *The Rocky Horror Picture Show*, with the lips, was produced to tie in with which 1975 blockbuster movie?

A) The Exorcist
B) Star Wars
C) Jaws
D) The Godfather

124. Regarding Eddie and Rocky, what does Frank say is the mistake he made with them?

A) Not giving them a brain
B) Splitting a brain between the two of them
C) Giving them a heightened libido
D) Giving them too many muscles

125. What does Frank tell Magenta she will receive in abundance?

A) Zero
B) Nil
C) Nothing
D) Zilch

126. Out of the following titles, which one is a REAL TITLE of a porn parody of *The Rocky Horror Picture Show*?

A) The Body Horror Picture Show
B) The Cocky Boner Porn Show
C) The Foxy Daughter Tit-Sure Show
D) The Rocki Whore Picture Show

127. In reference to the upcoming floor show that Frank has spoken about, what does The Criminologist say it's clear it wasn't going to be?

A) A walk in the park
B) A picnic
C) A breeze
D) A turkey shoot

128. Who is the first character to perform in the song *Rose Tint My World* during the floor show?

A) Rocky
B) Janet
C) Columbia
D) Brad

129. Whilst filming scenes involving the swimming pool, which of the performers caught pneumonia?

A) Tim Curry
B) Barry Bostwick
C) Little Nell
D) Susan Sarandon

130. What best describes the seating in the theatre where the floor show is performed?

A) Striped deck chairs
B) Wooden park bench chairs
C) Leather armchairs
D) Black barber chairs

131. Which American film studio logo is revealed when Frank begins to sing *Fanfare/Don't Dream It, Be It*?

A) Columbia Pictures
B) 20th Century Fox
C) Hammer Film Productions
D) RKO Radio Pictures

132. Which American actress stars as Dr. Frank-N-Furter in *The Rocky Horror Picture Show: Let's Do the Time Warp Again* (2016)?

A) Dominique Jackson

B) Michaela Jaé Rodriguez
C) Laverne Cox
D) Alexandra Billings

133. What is written upon the lifebuoy that Frank sits in whilst singing *Don't Dream It, Be It* in the swimming pool?

A) Mary Celeste
B) S.S. Titanic
C) Santa Maria
D) Queen Elizabeth 2

134. When Dr. Scott joins in during *Don't Dream It, Be It,* he says he has to be strong and try to hang on, or his mind may well - *what?*

A) Slip
B) Stop
C) Snip
D) Snap

135. How many times does Frank sing "My" at the beginning of *Wild and Untamed Thing?*

A) 12
B) 13
C) 14
D) 15

136. What does Riff Raff tell Magenta to prepare at the end of *Wild and Untamed Thing?*

A) The Transom Beam
B) The Transfix Beam
C) The Tranship Beam
D) The Transit Beam

137. What are audience members supposed to throw at screenings/productions of *Rocky Horror* when Frank sings the line, "Cards for sorrow, cards for pain," during *I'm Going Home*?

A) Playing cards
B) Birthday cards
C) Tarot cards
D) Estate Agent business cards

138. What is Columbia doing throughout the song, *I'm Going Home*?

A) Tap dancing
B) Shining a spotlight on Frank
C) Doing water aerobics in the pool
D) Sitting in one of the audience seats

139. Which classic horror character does Magenta's hair and makeup style resemble when she's in her spacesuit?

A) Vampira
B) Lily Munster
C) Morticia Addams
D) The Bride of Frankenstein

140. Whose foot got accidentally stepped on by a stiletto heel during *Wild and Untamed Thing*?

A) Tim Curry's
B) Little Nell's
C) Peter Hinwood's
D) Barry Bostwick's

141. How many ray beams shoot out Riff Raff's ray gun?

A) One
B) Two
C) Three
D) Four

142. Who played Frank-N-Furter in the first run of shows for the 50th Anniversary production of *The Rocky Horror Show* in Australia in 2023?

A) Craig McLachlan
B) Michael Ball
C) Daniel Abineri
D) Jason Donovan

143. What does Riff Raff say is the name of the planet and the galaxy that they're about to beam the entire house back to?

A) Planet Transgender in the galaxy of Transenstein
B) Planet Transsexual in the galaxy of Transylvania
C) Planet Transworld in the galaxy of Transducer
D) Planet Transtopia in the galaxy of Transacula

144. Which previously heard song do Riff Raff and Magenta reference when they talk about returning to their home planet?

A) The Time Warp
B) Sweet Transvestite
C) Science Fiction/Double Feature
D) Over at the Frankenstein Place

145. What is all Janet knows in the song *Superheroes*?

A) That still the beast is bleeding

B) That still the beast is needing
C) That still the beast is fleeing
D) That still the beast is feeding

146. Which role does Tim Curry play in *The Rocky Horror Picture Show: Let's Do the Time Warp Again*?

A) Dr. Scott
B) Ralph Hapschatt
C) The Criminologist
D) A Theatre Patron

147. What is the final shot in the movie before the end credits roll?

A) The castle blasting off into space
B) The Criminologist's illuminated globe
C) Brad, Janet, and Dr. Scott crawling on the floor outside
D) The lips from the beginning of the movie

148. In 2001, Richard O'Brien confirmed that he was working on a new sequel to *The Rocky Horror Picture Show* – what was the (unconfirmed) title of it?

A) The Rocky Horror Picture Show Part II
B) Rocky Horror: Back to the Frankenstein Place
C) Rocky Horror: The Second Coming
D) The Rocky Horror Double Feature

149. In the reprise of *Science Fiction/Double Feature* at the end of the movie, what is said about Frank?

A) He's created and killed his creature
B) He's made and mislaid his creature
C) He's had and gone his creature
D) He's built and lost his creature

150. After the reprise of *Science Fiction/Double Feature*, which song (in an instrumental version) plays over the rest of the end credits?

A) The Time Warp
B) Sweet Transvestite
C) Hot Patootie – Bless My Soul
D) Wild and Untamed Thing

THE ROCKY HORROR PICTURE SHOW

Answers

1) C - They Came from Denton High

2) C - Patricia Quinn's *(although the vocal is performed by Richard O'Brien. Quinn initially refused to star in the movie because of not being allowed to sing the opening track, which was always her song in the stage show, so the producers took her to see images of the costumes and sets for the film and she changed her mind because she thought they looked amazing)*

3) B – The Usherette *(the actress playing The Usherette will often play the character of Magenta, but not always. The character has also been known as Miss Strawberry Time, Trixie, and The Belasco Popcorn Girl)*

4) D - War of the Worlds

5) B - Denton Episcopalian Church

6) C - Eddie and Dr. Scott

7) A - She Got Hers Now He'll Get His

8) B - A pitchfork

9) C - Jonathan Adams *(Adams was the Narrator in the stage show and Dr. Scott in the movie)*

10) D - Be Just And Fear Not

11) B - A year or two

12) C - Steve Martin

13) C - Home

14) D - He's The Hero – That's Right, The Hero!!

15) A - A heart

16) B - Shown in black and white *(this was intended as an homage to The Wizard of Oz. A DVD/Blu-ray extra allows viewers to see it, roughly, how it was first intended – although the lips at the beginning were supposed to be red. There seems some confusion over whether the colour was supposed to kick in during The Time Warp, or upon the first appearance of Frank-N-Furter because the DVD extra has it on The Time Warp, but the filmmakers say it was supposed to be at the beginning of Sweet Transvestite – although it was only going to be Frank's lips in colour, going to full colour only at the end of the song)*

17) D - Mediocre

18) C - Elvis Presley

19) B - A coffin

20) D - Richard Hartley *(Hartley was a member of the original*

four-piece band for The Rocky Horror Show stage show in 1973 and went on to arrange the score for the film and its follow-up, Shock Treatment)
21) D - November
22) C - Tim Curry
23) B - The Denton Affair
24) B - Asshole for Brad, Slut for Janet
25) C - A chocolate bar
26) B - Three
27) D - Shadowcasts
28) A - President Nixon's resignation *(Nixon's 1974 resignation speech is heard playing. Some people have pointed out the continuity error that the speech is from August, but the film is supposed to be set in November – but maybe the radio was just replaying it!)*
29) B – Tim Curry *(Curry recounted the incident on a TV talk show saying, 'I went rather early on at the Waverly Theatre in New York, and they thought I was an imposter. And they threw me out! I thought it was enormous fun, I was having a ball – and then I got thrown out!" He wasn't in costume, though)*
30) C - Enter At Your Own Risk!!
31) D - Blackest night
32) C - Newspapers
33) B - In an upstairs window
34) C - Oakley Court *(now a luxury hotel)*
35) B - Hello
36) C - The Crystal Maze *(O'Brien hosted the show from 1990-1993. When O'Brien left, the new host was Ed Tudor-Pole, who had also played Riff Raff in The Rocky Horror Show – at the Piccadilly Theatre in London from July 1990 to June 1991)*
37) D - Rich weirdos
38) B - Richard O'Brien *(replacing Bruce Scott as Riff Raff)*
39) A - A feather duster
40) D - 12 o'clock *(midnight)*
41) C - It contained a real skeleton *(supposedly the skeleton of the Countess of Rosslyn's young Italian lover – she was so distraught after his death that she had his skeleton turned into the grisly coffin clock. It sold at auction in 2002 for £35,000)*

42) B - The pelvic thrust

43) B - Mona Lisa

44) C - Tenacious D

45) B - Christopher Biggins

46) D – The Madison

47) C - But by night I'm one hell of a lover

48) A – BOSS *(Frank also has a tattoo on his thigh with the number 4711 on it, which is a cologne (4711 Eau de Cologne). The number used to be used on all membership cards for The Rocky Horror Picture Show Official Fan Club. The number can also be seen on a microfilm file in Shock Treatment)*

49) D - Queen Elizabeth II

50) C – Water *(although, also correct if you said wine, because in the original screenplay it does say it's a wine dispenser, so it could also have been white wine that he threw)*

51) C - 3 seconds *(the pause is about 9 seconds in The Rocky Horror Picture Show: Let's Do the Time Warp Again (2016) and features the audience call back line, "Say it!" in the gap)*

52) D - Adrian Edmondson *(although he played Brad Majors in the 1990 West End run of the show, and was one of the Narrators in the 2015 Amnesty International production of the show at the Playhouse Theatre, London)*

53) B - A Champagne bottle

54) C - Vice

55) D - The Lords of Salem *(as the character Megan. Zombie also named his 2014 concert film, The Zombie Horror Picture Show, after the movie and cast Barry Bostwick in a cameo role as the Narrator in 3 from Hell. Zombie's film House of 1000 Corpses was heavily influenced by Rocky Horror – being a more full-on horror version of a similar story)*

56) B - Biochemical research

57) A - Pink

58) C - Mick Jagger *(even though David Bowie isn't the correct answer, Frank-N-Furter's makeup design was created by Pierre La Roche who also created Bowie's Ziggy Stardust makeup. Bowie had also been considered for the role when the studio was contemplating using bigger stars in the film, rather than the cast from the stage production)*

59) B - Three more

60) A – The Hammer Films *(after Hammer sold Bray Studios in 1970 it was more sparingly used as a film studio but recently the new owners re-established it as a studio space. Mark Gatiss was delighted to be able to shoot some of his new BBC Dracula series at Bray Studios, saying, "It's amazing to be able to say that Count Dracula has finally come home")*

61) D - Oh Rocky!

62) C - The Revenge of Frankenstein *(the 1958 Hammer Film Production – the bandaged body was also a prop from the movie. When Frank is releasing the various colours of paint into the tank, he is doing them in the order of a rainbow. He was being shouted out directions by Production Designer Brian Thomson of which colour to use next, which is why you can see Tim Curry searching so intently for the correct colour)*

63) B - The Sword of Damocles

64) B - A belly button *(on account of Rocky being created and not born)*

65) D - He's okay

66) C – Superheroes *(based upon attending various screenings of the movie in America, producer Lou Adler had the song cut from US prints as he felt it was too downbeat and depressing for the end of the movie – preferring to have audiences leave on a high)*

67) A - Charles Atlas'

68) B - A Creation

69) D - Jerk

70) B – Clue *(as the butler, Wadsworth)*

71) C - BABY

72) D - Saturday Night Live *(Tim and Meat's One-Stop Rocky Horror Shop, aired in 1981)*

73) A - Adam Lambert

74) B - A saxophone

75) D - Russell Crowe *(he also played the Dr. Scott role – footage of his performance can be seen on YouTube)*

76) C - An ice pick

77) B - Rose petals *(other props used at screenings include water pistols, flashlights, rubber gloves, noisemakers, party hats, bells, cards and (more rarely) hot dogs and prunes)*

78) D - I'm a muscle fan
79) A - Vincent Price *(he was offered the role but couldn't accept it because of a scheduling conflict)*
80) B - Simply a figment of the imagination
81) D - Jack Nicholson and Danny DeVito
82) C - She pulls his wig off *(which is exactly what Brad does when he believes Frank is Janet)*
83) B - Richard O' Brien and Patricia Quinn
84) D - Mopping the floor
85) B - A candelabra
86) C - One of the Transylvania extras had previously appeared in The Wizard of Oz *(although their forces were sped up to make them sound a bit Munchkin-like — this was down to the fact that the film was supposed to play out like a dark version of The Wizard of Oz)*
87) A - His mother's grave
88) D - Jim Sharman *(Sharman also co-wrote the screenplay as well as directing and co-writing Shock Treatment)*
89) B - If only Dr. Scott was with us
90) D - The Sword of Damocles and Planet, Schmanet, Janet
91) A - From her petticoat
92) B - Using a hair dryer
93) A - Zoolander 2
94) C - More and Down
95) D - Film studios *(the shield the griffin statue holds represents Warner Bros; the eagle in the hall is Republic Pictures; Columbia's name and appearance after Columbia Pictures; MGM is represented by the snarling cat in the hall; The Criminologist's globe represents Universal Pictures; the gong represents The Rank Organisation; Columbia's Mickey Mouse ears for Disney and R.K.O. more blatantly during the floor show)*
96) B - Rocky
97) A - Once in a While *(it can be viewed in the Deleted Scenes on home video releases of the movie)*
98) D - You know this earthling?
99) C - Elvira's Haunted Hills
100) B - UFOs

101) A - A cigarette butt

102) C – Narrator *(a role that he reprised for the 1990/1991 West End Revival of the show)*

103) C - Triple Contact Electro Magnet

104) B - Three times

105) C – Pennywise *(in the 1990 TV Miniseries adaptation of Stephen King's It)*

106) B - Bonhomie

107) C - Virgins

108) A - Rocky picks up his glass of wine

109) D - Princess Diana *(Diana reportedly told Tim Curry, with a wicked smile, that the movie had, "Quite completed her education")*

110) B - Ketchup

111) A - The Criminologist

112) C - As a Midnight Movie *(the movie practically invented the Midnight Movie phenomenon, or certainly popularised it. The Rocky Horror Picture Show began its run at the Waverly Theatre in New York City in April 1976 and it wasn't long before audience members began shouting things out at the screen and throwing props. According to Rocky Horror Picture Show Fan Club president, Sal Piro, the very first person to shout at the screen was Louis Farese, a kindergarten teacher from Staten Island – he called out, "How strange was it?" when The Criminologist says, "I would like, if I may, to take you on a strange journey." Another very early line was, "Buy an umbrella, you cheap bitch!" when Janet uses a newspaper to shield from the rain. Owing to this audience participation, the movie went on to become one of the longest-running film releases in film history, continuing to play at movie theatres to this day)*

113) B - I'm out my hed

114) A - Christopher Biggins *(the Narrators were Stephen Fry, Ade Edmondson, Emma Bunton, Mel Giedroyc, Anthony Head, and Richard O'Brien. Although, Biggins has been the Narrator in tours of The Rocky Horror Show – including one of the shows I went to see)*

115) D – Janet *(closely followed by Frank who chases after her)*

116) B - David Bedella

117) A - A pencil

118) C – Phantoms *(they're credited as Transylvanians in the film)*

119) C - Sonic Transducer

120) B - Planet Hot Dog

121) C - Meat Loaf and Barry Bostwick

122) D - Rocky

123) C – Jaws *(featuring the tagline "A Different Set Of Jaws")*

124) B - Splitting a brain between the two of them

125) C - Nothing

126) D - The Rocki Whore Picture Show *(and it's very good… so I've been told)*

127) B - A picnic

128) C - Columbia

129) D - Susan Sarandon

130) A - Striped deck chairs

131) D - RKO Radio Pictures *(as: an RKO Radio Picture. Initially it was going to be a 20th Century Fox logo with the searchlight beams being built with big planks of plywood on strings that Columbia and Magenta would pull so that they would jerkily move on the stage)*

132) C - Laverne Cox

133) B - S.S. Titanic

134) D - Snap

135) C - 14

136) D - The Transit Beam

137) A - Playing cards *(although other types of cards have been known to be thrown, but generally it's playing cards)*

138) B - Shining a spotlight on Frank

139) D - The Bride of Frankenstein

140) D - Barry Bostwick's *(Susan Sarandon's heel caught his foot when she stepped back – Bostwick's look of pain is clearly captured in the movie)*

141) C - Three

142) D - Jason Donovan *(David Bedella took over the role in July 2023)*

143) B - Planet Transsexual in the galaxy of Transylvania

144) A - The Time Warp *("And our world will do The Time Warp again!")*

145) D - That still the beast is feeding

146) C - The Criminologist

147) B - The Criminologist's illuminated globe
148) C - Rocky Horror: The Second Coming *(Rocky Horror fans had given it the title, but it was never confirmed by O'Brien. The show would be set nine months after The Rocky Horror Show and would feature the story of Janet being pregnant with either Frank or Rocky's baby. Elements of the screenplay were taken from another unmade screenplay called Revenge of the Old Queen – I can still recall seeing a TV show where Richard O'Brien and Ade Edmondson were both guests. Edmondson was talking about the new Carry On movie (Carry on Columbus) that he was considering starring in, but when O'Brien mentioned he was going to make Revenge of the Old Queen, Ade appeared very interested and said he wanted to be in that movie instead. As it turned out, Ade never did appear in Carry on Columbus and, sadly, Revenge of the Old Queen didn't go into production)*
149) D - He's built and lost his creature
150) A - The Time Warp

DOUBLE DIFFICULT ROCKY HORROR
Questions

1. In which London theatre did _The Rocky Horror Show_ have its premiere performance in 1973?

A) King's Head Theatre
B) Bromley Little Theatre
C) Royal Vauxhall Tavern
D) Royal Court Theatre

2. During the taking of the group photograph at Ralph and Betty's wedding, how many people are present in the photo?

A) 14
B) 15
C) 16
D) 17

3. What is the newspaper that Janet is seen reading as she and Brad are driving through the rain on their way to see Dr. Scott?

A) The Columbus Dispatch
B) The Plain Dealer
C) Denton Daily News
D) The Cincinnati Enquirer

4. Who was the original Rocky Horror actor in the 1973 stage production of the show?

A) Kim Milford
B) Wayne Pygram
C) Jay Hackett
D) Rayner Bourton

5. When The Criminologist turns to Eddie's mugshot in the file, what is his booking ID number?

A) 63230
B) 250342
C) 274306
D) 190446

6. In the original *The Rocky Horror Picture Show* film trailer, which actress performs as the lips?

A) Rhea Ruggiero
B) Pamela Obermeyer
C) Annabelle Leventon
D) Peggy Ledger

7. What was the original title of the script that O'Brien wrote in 1978 as a film sequel to *The Rocky Horror Picture Show,* which was eventually renamed *Rocky Horror Shows His Heels*?

A) The Curse of Rocky
B) The Curse of the Baby
C) The Curse of the Hot Dog
D) The Curse of Transylvania

8. Who wrote the 1980 novelisation of *The Rocky Horror Picture Show*, named *The Official Rocky Horror Picture Show Movie Novel*?

A) Phillip Larner
B) Daniel Riding
C) Richard J. Anobile
D) James Lefebure

9. Which performer has starred in *The Rocky Horror Show* stage version more times than any other actor?

A) Tim Curry
B) David Bedella
C) Richard Meek
D) Kristian Lavercombe

10. Who provided the singing voice for the character of Rocky Horror in *The Rocky Horror Picture Show*?

A) Peter Marinker
B) Trevor White
C) James Keach
D) Marc Martel

11. What is the name of the Michelangelo painting that appears on the tiles of the swimming pool when Frank sings *Don't Dream It, Be It*?

A) The Last Judgment
B) The Dream of Human Life
C) The Creation of the Sun, Moon, and Vegetation
D) The Creation of Adam

12. Which type of clothing are audience goers not supposed to wear at screenings or theatre performances of *Rocky Horror*?

A) Leather jackets
B) Football tops
C) Striped sweatshirts
D) Hawaiian shirts

13. After directing *The Rocky Horror Picture Show*, Jim Sharman directed a 1976 movie that starred Nell Campbell – what is the title of it?

A) Arcade
B) Summer of Secrets
C) Roll Up
D) Shirley Thompson vs. the Aliens

14. What is Richard O'Brien's birthname?

A) Richard Timothy Smith
B) Richard Harry Dutton
C) Richard Iris Davenport
D) Richard Terry Bradbury

15. Which American actor was the original choice to play Frank-N-Furter in the 1973 stage production of *The Rocky Horror Show*?

A) Reg Livermore
B) Max Phipps
C) Jonathan Kramer
D) David James

16. A 1995 album recording of *The Rocky Horror Show* featured Christopher Lee as The Narrator – which legendary rock star performed Eddie's song, renamed as *Whatever Happened to Saturday Night*?

A) Elton John
B) Brian May
C) Robert Plant
D) Bruce Dickinson

17. Tim Curry was born in the same town as me, Warrington, but in which civil parish?

A) Great Sankey
B) Birchwood
C) Poulton-with-Fearnhead
D) Grappenhall

18. Which song did Tim Curry perform in his audition, which successfully landed him the role of Frank-N-Furter in the original stage show?

A) Hello Mary Lou
B) Gimme Some Lovin'
C) Tutti Frutti
D) (You're So Square) Baby I Don't Care

19. Who is the only performer to appear in *The Rocky Horror Picture Show, Shock Treatment*, and *The Rocky Horror Picture Show: Let's Do the Time Warp Again* – as well as the original stage production of *The Rocky Horror Show*?

A) Tim Curry
B) Richard O'Brien
C) Patricia Quinn
D) Little Nell

20. Responsible for creating some of the most iconic costumes in history, who was the costume designer for both the original *Rocky Horror* stage show and movie?

A) Marit Allen
B) Sue Blane
C) Van Smith
D) Sue Yelland

21. Which celebrated British artist created the artwork for the Arrow Video Blu-ray release of *Shock Treatment*?

A) Bill Gold
B) Robert Gleason
C) Graham Humphreys
D) Roger Kastel

22. What exactly is the mistake in the Misprint Ending featured in the Bonus Features on home video releases of the movie?

A) There are no end credits, just a black screen
B) Superheroes has the wrong audio
C) All of the audio is out of sync
D) The scenes are edited in the wrong order

23. Tim Curry reprised his role as Dr. Frank-N-Furter in a live table reading of *The Rocky Horror Picture Show* in 2020 – what was this livestream event in aid of?

A) The Texas Democratic Party
B) The Democratic Party of Wisconsin
C) The Ohio Democratic Party
D) District of Columbia Democratic State Committee

24. Whose lips feature on the theatrical posters for *The Rocky Horror Picture Show*?

A) Yasmin Pettigrew's
B) Rayner Bourton's
C) Lorelei Shark's
D) Lindsay Ingram's

25. Which small role did the world's most well-known *Rocky Horror* fan and founder and president of The Rocky Horror Picture Show Fan Club, Sal Piro, have in *The Rocky Horror Picture Show: Let's Do the Time Warp Again?*

A) Skeleton Crew Dancer
B) Vicar
C) Usher
D) The Photographer

DOUBLE DIFFICULT ROCKY HORROR

Answers

1) D - Royal Court Theatre *(in the 63-seat Theatre Upstairs, now known as the Jerwood Theatre Upstairs. It was soon transferred to the Chelsea Classic Cinema from August 1973 to October 1973 before staying for a much longer run at the King's Road Theatre from November 1973 to March 1979)*

2) C - 16

3) B - The Plain Dealer *(a real major newspaper from Cleveland, Ohio)*

4) D - Rayner Bourton *(Bourton wrote a book in 2009 about his experiences in The Rocky Horror Show called The Rocky Horror Show: As I Remember It)*

5) C - 274306

6) A - Rhea Ruggiero

7) B - The Curse of the Baby

8) C - Richard J. Anobile *(the credit reads: Edited and adapted by Richard J. Anobile, Screenplay by Jim Sharman and Richard O'Brien)*

9) D - Kristian Lavercombe *(to date, Lavercombe has performed in the show over 2400 times (setting a world record), usually as Riff Raff, but he's also played the Narrator, Brad Majors and Frank-N-Furter. At the time of writing, he is still performing in The Rocky Horror Show current 2023 UK tour as Riff Raff)*

10) B - Trevor White *(White was a member of the 60s/70s British rock/pop group, Sounds Incorporated. He would go on to star in the Australian production of Jesus Christ Superstar as Jesus and would appear on the album of the Original Australian Cast Recording of the musical)*

11) D - The Creation of Adam *(part of the Sistine Chapel's ceiling)*

12) C - Striped sweatshirts *(supposedly, there is a brief moment in the movie when crew members wearing striped shirts are caught on camera — although this is actually an urban legend started by Dave Freeman in TimeWarp — The Virgins Guide to Rocky Horror. Dave addressed this on Facebook by saying, 'It was a visual gag from a photo I took over thirty years ago. The original guide allows the stripes reference to work because it has my images in. The moment it gets quoted without the image it becomes a seed for urban legends. I had to explain it to Rocky Radio for one of their shows as various theories*

were popping up on the origin of the 'stripes ban' whereas in reality it was just a pun on the photo and there is no ban" — thanks to Angela Davies for sharing this information with me)

13) B - Summer of Secrets

14) A - Richard Timothy Smith *(he used his mother's maiden name as a surname as there already was an actor named Richard Smith)*

15) C - Jonathan Kramer *(O'Brien said, "Kramer was in the running - more than in the running. We just imagined Jonathan was going to do it and Tim walked into the room and auditioned for Jim (Sharman) and by the time I came back, that had changed in half an hour." Previously, Kramer had appeared in the 1969 classic movie, Midnight Cowboy and sadly died in 1976 aged just 30)*

16) B - Brian May *(the Queen star also provided the guitar parts on the track, obviously!)*

17) D – Grappenhall *(its full title is Grappenhall and Thelwall. Curry attended Lymm High School in Warrington and his mother was a secretary/receptionist at the now closed down Grappenhall Hall School)*

18) C - Tutti Frutti *(the 1955 Little Richard song)*

19) D - Little Nell *(she was uncredited as The Criminologist's Assistant in The Rocky Horror Picture Show: Let's Do the Time Warp Again)*

20) B - Sue Blane *(she also designed the costumes for Shock Treatment)*

21) C - Graham Humphreys *(best known for his iconic horror posters of the Nightmare on Elm Street and Evil Dead movies)*

22) A - Superheroes has the wrong audio *(we see Brad and Janet crawling around in the smoky space where the castle once stood, but the audio is The Criminologist's speaking part from the end of the song)*

23) B - The Democratic Party of Wisconsin

24) C - Lorelei Shark's *(ironically, the poster that Playboy model Shark modelled for was the one with the tagline A Different Set Of Jaws, a reference to the movie, Jaws. Shark says that she was paid $120 for modelling as the lips)*

25) D - The Photographer *(Sal sadly passed away in January 2023. He also appeared in Shock Treatment as a man using a*

SHOCK TREATMENT
Questions

1. Before the script was rewritten as *Shock Treatment*, what was the title of Richard O'Brien's initial, more direct, sequel to *The Rocky Horror Picture Show*?

A) Rocky Shock Horror
B) Rocky Horror Shows His Heels
C) Rocky Returns
D) Over at the Frank-N-Furter Place

2. Seen in the opening number, *Denton, U.S.A.*, which character (and performer) is the only one to reprise their role from *The Rocky Horror Picture Show*?

A) Magenta played by Patricia Quinn
B) The Criminologist played by Charles Gray
C) Ralph Hapschatt played by Jeremy Newson
D) Riff Raff played by Richard O'Brien

3. *Shock Treatment*'s Brad Majors actor Cliff De Young had been initially sought for a role in *The Rocky Horror Picture Show* – who was he going to play before a scheduling conflict meant he had to drop out?

A) Rocky Horror
B) Eddie
C) The Criminologist
D) Brad

4. What is the name of the DTV gameshow that Bert Schnick (Barry Humphries) is the host of, which Brad and Janet become his unwitting contestants on?

A) Marriage Maze
B) Happy Homes
C) Faith Factory
D) Denton Dossier

5. During the song *Bitchin' in the Kitchen*, what is NOT one of the household appliances mentioned?

A) Refrigerator
B) Percolator
C) Blender
D) Lawnmower

6. Which popular British comedy actor portrayed the character "Rest Home" Ricky?

A) Ade Edmondson
B) Nigel Planer
C) Rik Mayall
D) Peter Richardson

7. What is the name of the soap opera and mental hospital that is central to the story in the movie?

A) Dentonville
B) Dentonvale
C) Dentondale
D) Dentonton

8. For which character was Barry Humphries (Bert Schnick) best known for portraying?

A) Dame Edna Everage
B) Lily Savage
C) Divine
D) Edna Turnblad

9. What is the tagline on the theatrical poster for *Shock Treatment*?

A) Some Lines Shouldn't Be Crossed
B) It's Been 6 Years. Time For Your Check-Up!

C) So Much Fun – You'll Never Recover
D) Trust Me, I'm A Doctor

10. Throughout the movie, Brad is mostly kept locked up in a padded cell – what is the shape of the cage he is imprisoned in?

A) Square
B) Circular
C) Triangular
D) Rectangular

11. Prior to *Shock Treatment*, which cult Brian De Palma movie did Jessica Harper (Janet Majors) star in, which impressed the producers enough to cast her?

A) Phantom of the Paradise
B) Sisters
C) Obsession
D) Dressed to Kill

12. What is Bert Schnick cured of during the course of the movie?

A) His deafness
B) His broken leg
C) His blindness
D) His bad back

13. As sung by Cosmo (Richard O'Brien) in the song of the same name, what is the dress that he makes for Janet?

A) Little Red Dress
B) Little Pink Dress
C) Little Green Dress
D) Little Black Dress

14. What is written upon the sign seen throughout the movie at the base of the audience seating area?

A) It's Good To Be Home On DTV
B) It's Gotta Be DTV
C) Get Into DTV
D) DTV – Denton's First 24-Hour Channel

15. Fully embracing her newfound fame, which song does Janet perform live in the studio before the audience?

A) Carte Blanche
B) Looking For Trade
C) In My Own Way
D) Me of Me

16. What is the name of the character played by Little Nell in *Shock Treatment*?

A) Nurse Wright
B) Nurse Struthers
C) Nurse Ansalong
D) Nurse Lapsey

17. Where is the movie's title track, *Shock Treatment*, performed?

A) In front of the studio audience
B) In Brad's padded cell
C) In the wardrobe room
D) In the dining room

18. Unlike *The Rocky Horror Show*, *Shock Treatment* was never performed on the stage until 2015 when there was finally a theatrical production...

TRUE or FALSE?

19. When the band introduce themselves to Janet, what do they say their name is?

A) Dr. Teeth and the Electric Mayhem
B) Marvin Berry and the Starlighters
C) Barry Jive and the Uptown Five
D) Oscar Drill and the Bits

20. Visible in the wardrobe room in *Shock Treatment* is a prop from *The Rocky Horror Picture Show* – what is it?

A) The coffin clock
B) The American Gothic painting
C) Riff Raff's ray gun
D) Rocky's birth tank

21. Looking on a computer, what does Betty Hapschatt (Ruby Wax) discover about Cosmo and Nation McKinley?

A) That they're character actors
B) That they're aliens
C) That they're undercover police
D) That they're escaped mental asylum patients

22. What is Janet crowned in the new reality TV show, Faith Factory?

A) Miss Denton
B) Miss Mental Health
C) Miss TV Star of the Year

D) Miss Flavor of the Week

23. Who is it revealed that Farley Flavors really is?

A) Brad's father
B) Brad's uncle
C) Brad's twin brother
D) Brad's twin sister

24. What are the audience members given as they are led out of the studio?

A) Baseball caps
B) Straitjackets
C) Pills
D) ID badges

25. What is the movie's closing song sung by Brad, Janet, Betty, and Judge Oliver Wright (Charles Gray)?

A) Duel Duet
B) Breaking Out
C) In My Own Way
D) Anyhow, Anyhow

SHOCK TREATMENT
Answers

85

1) B - Rocky Horror Shows His Heels *(which was then rewritten as The Brad and Janet Show, which ultimately became Shock Treatment)*

2) C - Ralph Hapschatt played by Jeremy Newson

3) D — Brad *(he was the original choice for Brad Majors in The Rocky Horror Picture Show — funnily enough, Barry Bostwick was approached to reprise his role as Brad in Shock Treatment, but had to back down because of a scheduling conflict too)*

4) A - Marriage Maze

5) D - Lawnmower

6) C - Rik Mayall

7) B - Dentonvale

8) A - Dame Edna Everage *(and also as Sir Les Patterson)*

9) D - Trust Me, I'm A Doctor

10) B - Circular

11) A - Phantom of the Paradise *(Susan Sarandon had also been approached but there wasn't enough money in the budget to pay her, as she'd become a bigger star in the 80s)*

12) C - His blindness *(of course, it's debatable if he was ever blind in the first place)*

13) D - Little Black Dress

14) B - It's Gotta Be DTV *(the movie was ultimately set entirely inside a television studio on account of the Screen Actors Guild going on strike. The filmmakers had wished to make the movie in Denton, Texas, and had even scouted locations over there with the intention of shooting the movie on location. However, the strike halted their plans and because of the small window of availability of their cast and crew they had no other viable option other than to make some changes to the script and shoot the whole movie inside Lee International Studios in London)*

15) D - Me of Me

16) C - Nurse Ansalong

17) B - In Brad's padded cell

18) True *(theatre director, and Shock Treatment fan, Benji Sperring, had longed to bring Shock Treatment to the stage, although Richard O'Brien was more reluctant. O'Brien (who became involved as a producer) finally relented with the stipulation that it be performed in a*

very small theatre, much like how the original Rocky Horror Show had. It ended up at the 110-seat King's Head Theatre in 2015 from 17ᵗʰ April to 6ᵗʰ June)

19) D - Oscar Drill and the Bits *(future popstar Sinitta plays Frankie – one of the Bits)*

20) B - The American Gothic painting

21) A - That they're character actors

22) B - Miss Mental Health

23) C - Brad's twin brother

24) B - Straitjackets

25) D - Anyhow, Anyhow *(which contains a verse of Denton U.S.A.)*

THE ROCKY HORROR PICTURE SHOW
Filming Locations

Taken from The Magic Geekdom's *Rocky Horror Picture Show Filming Locations in Windsor, England* video (2022)

Please Like and Subscribe to Jeremy and Cara!

YouTube – youtube.com/themagicgeekdom
Facebook – www.facebook.com/ themagicgeekdom
Twitter – www.twitter.com/magicgeekdom
Instagram – instagram.com/ themagicgeekdom
TikTok - @themagicgeekdom

The Frankenstein Place - a wide exterior of Oakley Court in Windsor, England. Aside from the missing dome, it appears just like it did in the movie

The window where Riff Raff sings his part in Over at the Frankenstein Place

Another angle of the front of the Frankenstein Place – although, it should be noted that these establishing shots of the building are actually the back of Oakley Court

On the other side of the building – the front entrance to Oakley Court

The front entrance to Oakley Court where Brad and Janet are greeted by Riff Raff

A closer view of one of the gargoyles at the entrance, which can be clearly seen in the movie

The door where Riff Raff says "Hello" to Brad and Janet

The hallway and the stairs that are featured prominently in the movie

The stained-glass windows inside the hallway that can be seen behind Brad and Janet when they arrive at the castle

A closer view of the stairs that Magenta first appears on

The area where the coffin clock stood, seen during The Time Warp

The reception area next to the dining hall where Riff Raff dances around at the beginning of The Time Warp

The ceiling in the reception where the elevator was constructed for the movie

Reverse angle on the reception area where the beginning of The Time Warp is performed, and where the elevator once stood

The doors in the dining area that Brad and Janet stand in front of during The Time Warp

The area outside Oakley Court where Rocky was seen running after briefly escaping from the castle

*At the side of Oakley Court, where Brad, Janet and Dr. Scott exit at
the end of the movie and perform Superheroes*

The neighbouring Bray Studios where some of the interior sets were built

An aerial photo of Oakley Court

*And the delightful Cara and Jeremy from The Magic Geekdom outside
Oakley Court*

A STRANGE JOURNEY

By

Killian H. Gore and Phoenix Hinkley

The murder mystery night at Oakley Court should have been a blast, were it not for the fact that I was murdered for real.

It doesn't matter, of course. I'm not human in the first place, so I'm still here to tell the tale. It only bothered me because all I wanted was to take part in a fun event at an amazing location. I believe it was used in some Hammer horror movies and a cult musical called *The Rocky Horror Picture Show*, which I haven't seen yet but it sounds absolutely marvellous, and when (and if) I return to Earth, I'll have to make sure to check it out. The audience participation events sound wild!

I'm not totally humanoid in form, naturally, but our Vanbrienian brains are able to manipulate what human beings see so we can appear more humanlike to them. Admittedly, we're not that far off from what you look like, we do have a lot of similarities. We have the same two legs and arms and hands and feet and all that, but we are green – and, yes, I know that's such a terrible cliché, but the whole little green men thing has its basis in fact, as a lot of clichés do. We're not little, though – average human height, and we have three eyes, which you lot don't. And, not wanting to sound crude, but our toilet bits are far more user-friendly. Let's just say we don't have the same requirement to use all that toilet paper that you filthy animals do.

I'd always been curious about these murder mystery evenings that are quite popular on your planet. They seem like such an unusual activity to enjoy – why on Earth is murder the basis of a fun night out? I just had to find out, and the one I saw advertised at Oakley Court looked like the perfect one to take part in, as I really loved the look of the grand old building.

Things did get off to a bad start so I should have known it wasn't going to be the best of evenings. My car broke down and, just like it always seems to on Earth, in the area you call England, it was raining. I got out to inspect the car, not truly knowing what I was doing (does anyone, really?) and noticed that the front tyre was deflated. If I'd bothered to check a bit further at that point I'd have noticed that it wasn't the only flat tyre, but the rain was coming down pretty heavily so I made the choice to leave it for now and deal with it later. I know how to change tyres, by the way – we're a highly intelligent race. How do you think we got here in the first place?

Thankfully, I wasn't too far from the mansion, so I grabbed a newspaper I'd bought earlier in the day and held it over my head as I walked the half mile or so over to the Gothic wonder that is Oakley Court.

Owing to the breakdown, I was the last guest to arrive and I felt this immediately got me off on the wrong foot with the twenty other participants, all of whom, I should add, were clearly couples. I was the only singleton amongst them. Maybe their quizzical looks upon my arrival were more intended to imply *where's your other half?* rather than *why are you late and holding a damp newspaper?*

There was a drink waiting for me on the table but it was nothing more exciting than water – ironic considering what I'd just walked in from. I chose to leave it where it was and picked up the *Welcome* leaflet instead that explained who the *staff* at the hotel were – the actors, in other words, and the suspects for the murder mystery that was hopefully going to get up and running soon. I couldn't bear the sneaky, fleeting glances in my direction for much longer.

Thankfully, it wasn't much longer at all as the Butler actor, who must have been playing the dual role of administrator, clocked my arrival, ticked something in a notebook and promptly went about striding confidently over to us all.

"Ladies and Gentlemen…" (*already goofing up, you're forgetting aliens*) "… welcome to Oakley Court. I will be your host for the night, my name is Timothy, and I am the butler here at this wonderful old hotel. We will begin with a free round…" (*erm, we've paid for this, Timothy?*) "… of drinks, which will be supplied by our two lovely waitresses, Mary, and Colleen, who will be around momentarily to take your orders. Now, are there any questions?"

"No, but I could murder a drink," some joker with an extraordinarily large moustache said from one of the tables. I could sense from Timothy's slightly sunken demeanour that he'd heard this joke so many times it was impossible to muster the enthusiasm to act amused. The same could not be said of the participants, who greeted the gag with more than enough zeal to completely cloak Timothy's lack of it.

"Very good sir," came his sardonic response as he clicked his fingers and conjured Mary and Colleen, neither of whom headed in the direction of the sore thumb singleton on the far table. I busied myself with the Welcome leaflet again and perused the names of the upcoming suspects and their tiny bios.

Timothy Adams – The Butler (Delusions of grandeur)
Mary Farr– Waitress #1 (Girlfriend of Brian)
Coleen Newson – Waitress #2 (Secretly dating Brian)
Edward Gray– The Bartender (Owner of a new Porsche)
Susan Curry – The Head Chef (Ex-drug addict)
Barry Biggins – The Sous-Chef (Once stole a motorcycle)
Jeremy Hinwood – Kitchen Helper (Big serial killer fan)
Brian White – Trainee Chef (Unreliable and unfaithful)
Hilary Quinn – The Receptionist (Used to be the manager)
Charles White – The Hotel Manager (Very suspicious of everyone)

Without knowing how these things play out, I wasn't entirely sure how all these characters were to come into our lives. All I really knew about the murder mystery phenomenon was the cliché that the butler did it. Just as my mind was about to wander…

"Would you like to join us?" a kind voice from the table next to me said, finally accepting that I'd definitely come here alone, and a wet husband wasn't about to splash down next to me.

Why not? I thought. It would snub the pity glares at least.

"Oh, yes. Yes. Thank you very much. I always feel like such an alien at any public events." I'd have winked at the audience if this were a play.

"I'm Sadie and this is my husband, Christopher."

"Enchanté, I'm Aileen," don't laugh.

Sadie made the choice to order Champagne for everyone when Coleen came over to the table and after she toddled off we casually flipped through the menus that she'd brought whilst making the smallest of small talk. I must admit I got a little distracted by the menu, checking to see if anything contained rice. For whatever reason, rice is deadly to us. One of our silly little foibles on your planet.

We wouldn't need to make a great deal more small talk as the story was soon to enfold around us when a mock argument between the Bartender and the Hotel Manager broke out as we all listened intently for potential clues. It would appear the tills were down and the Hotel Manager was asking how did the Bartender manage to buy such an expensive new car. It didn't make a whole lot of sense really as such an argument would occur behind closed doors in real life, but then this wasn't real life – or was it? There was something quite "off" about Edward the Bartender, in terms of his performance I mean. He seemed more natural acting compared to the rather over the top performances from the other cast members. Either he was just a bad actor or not an actor at all.

As I, Sadie and Christopher munched down our rather first rate three course meal (rice-free, thankfully) more such scenes intruded around us. We heard arguments in the kitchen, the two waitresses arguing over Brian the Trainee Chef, and the Butler and the Receptionist plotting to run their own hotel - it was all compellingly entertaining but so much information to take in. Where was it all leading?

Well, to murder, obviously. We were informed that the Hotel Manager had been found dead at the foot of the stairs after we'd finished our sticky toffee puddings. Oooh — the plot thickens! Stabbed to death. Wonderful!

With dinner consumed and more drinks (now at an extra cost and no longer of the Champagne variety) ordered, we all took to our Welcome leaflets to study the characters and chat about our early theories. Clearly the Butler and Receptionist seemed the most obvious suspects — killing the Hotel Manager so that they could take over running the hotel.

Of course, what I had failed to fully acknowledge through the proceedings was that Edward the Bartender had looked over in my direction more times than was natural. Curious looks, suspicious looks, studying looks. I swear that at one point he held up his phone for a moment. Taking a little snap of me, perhaps?

Sometimes, though it is incredibly rare, photographs or video footage of my type can reveal our true form. Usually the same theory applies that humans will still only see another human, regardless of it being a secondary source. But perhaps this was one of those incredibly rare cases — or maybe he had some exotic new TikTok filter that transcended our psychological guise. Was Edward aware that an alien sat amongst the diners? He certainly was excelling in making me feel uncomfortable.

"Ladies and Gentlemen, I have just been informed that the road to the hotel has become flooded... " *(did these guys provide that bloody rain, or was that just a lucky ad lib?)* "... the police are trying their very best to get up to the hotel as soon as they can, but until then we must all sit tight until they arrive. We believe some of you do have an interest in true crime," he said with a knowing smile that got a wave of giggles from the murder mystery enthusiasts, "So if you have any theories, do feel free to speculate. This isn't Twitter, so nobody will mock your armchair detective skills here," Timothy said, eliciting another laugh from the crowd.

Of my new friends, Sadie and Christopher, it was clear who the quiet one was as Sadie and I ran through our theories. Christopher just kept waving the waitresses over for more drinks – always a Scotch, always neat, always doubles. Clearly he'd been dragged out here by Sadie on the promise that she'd drive and he could get totally plastered.

"I can't see what the two waitresses and Brian have to do with all this, they seem in their own little…"

"Ménage à trois?" I offered, lowering the tone in a misjudged, smutty direction.

"Well… I don't think they're…" Sadie seemed too polite to finish the sentence. I only wanted to see what it would have done to her facial expression. I'm rather fascinated by human emotions.

"But wait. The surnames. Look. Brian and Charles have the same surname – White. The Trainee Chef and Hotel Manager could be related?" I suggested.

"It's quite a common name…"

"They're fictional names. It's a script!" Sadie was clearly never keen to accept this was all make believe.

"But yes, it's possible. What could it mean, though?" Sadie said with a puzzled frown.

"Either Coleen or Mary could have offed the hotel manager, maybe they confronted him about Brian and things turned ugly?"

"Yeah, he could have gotten angry at them and a nasty accident ended up happening."

"An accident?"

"Can there be two murderers at these things? And can the murders be accidental?" Like I said, I had no idea how murder mystery evenings worked.

As the night went on, we were encouraged to have

more of a wander around the rooms in the hotel – well, the lower floor rooms. The kitchen, the bar, the entrance hall, not up to the bedrooms, but we were allowed to see the bloodied sheet that was placed over Charles at the bottom of the stairs. He was shoved over to the side a bit, so that the hotel guest could still traipse up and down them without tripping over a faux corpse.

"Do you think he's actually under there? The actor?" I asked Sadie.

She didn't seem as keen to break character as me and so whispered her response, "It's probably a statue or a dummy or something."

I wanted to give it a harsh little kick with my pointy shoes to see if he screamed "Owwwww!" but I refrained.

"Come on, Aileen," Sadie said, grabbing me by the arm as she and I continued our investigation, leaving her hubby with his more liquidy friend, and entered the kitchen where… and this was quite a shocker… Susan the Head Chef was shooting up in the pantry! I kid you not! I desperately wanted to laugh as her performance was so dreadful as she fumbled with all the finesse of a pantomime horse, throwing the needle into a tub of carrots upon clocking us.

"Oh! You took me by surprise. Did you both enjoy your meals tonight?" Clearly Susan wasn't an actual chef as her whites were whiter than Charles and Brian's shared surname. The real kitchen team were probably tucked up their beds by now.

"Yes, it was lovely, thank you." Sadie offered. "I even asked for an extra slice of that beautiful pork." Which is true – she did. Two extra slices to be pedantic.

"So, where were you when Charles was killed?" I blurted out, acting like Sherlock Holmes all of a sudden – the Benedict Cumberbatch version (a fellow alien, I might add).

"I was in here. Jeremy was with me." I took out the leaflet. Jeremy: Big serial killer fan. Hmm, interesting. Was she covering for him? He could be a drug dealer who had supplied Susan with some junk in exchange for keeping schtum about murdering Charles. I pointed at Jeremy's name in the leaflet to Sadie and gave her a knowing look, which was reciprocated.

"How much of a serial killer fan is Jeremy?" Sadie asked Susan. It seemed like an excruciatingly lame question. What did she expect by way of retort? *Oh, he's a really big serial killer fan?!*

"Oh, he's a really big serial killer fan." For God's sake.

I wanted to leave, but Sadie chatted some more with Susan before having more of a search in the kitchen – hoping to find the bloody knife stashed somewhere, I assumed. Although it would be a pretty reckless place to leave the murder weapon. I'd have eaten it. We can consume metal, so I have that going for me.

Comically, there really was a bloodied knife in the kitchen, right next to a bottle of tomato sauce – the only items left out after the real kitchen team had obviously cleaned up. Barry Biggins, the sous chef was pretending to wipe up the area as we approached him.

"Wait. Let me check that knife. Is that really tomato ketchup on there? Don't touch it!" Jesus! Sadie was really taking this seriously – was she about to dust for prints?

"I spilled some when I was cleaning up," Barry said.

"How do you spill ketchup?" Good question, Sadie. It has to be squeezed out of the bottle. I'd have added a query about what ketchup was doing here in the kitchen anyway. That was surely more of a dining area adornment.

"I accidentally caught the bottle with the knife and it went all over the place." Yeah. I'll buy that. A little far-fetched, but possible. Good save, Barry.

We went back to check on Sadie's husband, who was now chatting with another husband – chatting with much slurring, the pair of them.

"Gots the killers yets my loves?" I'm thinking he was probably seeing two of his wife rather than me stood next to her.

"We're thinking Jeremy at the moment," Sadie said, plonking herself down on a different chair from her original one (hubby's drinking pal was now in that one).

"Who's Jeremy?"

"Kitchen helper – a big serial killer fan."

"How tall?" Hubby's new friend quipped. No one reacted.

"Yeps. Sounds likes hims thens," Hubby said, finishing his fortieth Scotch.

"Could I have your attention please, ladies and gentlemen?" Timothy interrupted over the lively dining room. "Is everyone here? I need everyone. All of the staff. Everyone, please."

On cue, the rest of the performers spilled into the room from their assorted locations, where they'd probably been poised for a couple of minutes waiting for this prompt. Timothy coolly waited at the bar for his acting buddies to join him.

"Good. Now. Is anyone missing?"

We all looked around the room, then down at our leaflets.

"Hang on… Hilary. We never went to see the receptionist, Hilary. She's not here," Sadie whispered to me, a little loudly.

"What was that? Is there somebody missing?" Timothy bellowed over to our table.

"The manager," Hubby sniffed, with a private guffaw.

"Yes. Hilary, the receptionist," Sadie confidentially emitted, shadowing her husband's grim wisecrack.

There were murmurs around the room. Others had begun to notice one of the cast had been mysteriously absent during the latter half of the evening.

"That's right, ladies and gentlemen," Timothy, quite bizarrely for England, pulled out a handgun and pointed it at all of us.

The hotel's front doors swung open. It was Hilary dressed all in leathers – well, we didn't know it was immediately Hilary as she was wearing a motorcycle helmet, which she theatrically proceeded to remove before tousling her hair with her most femme fatale swagger and a forced evil glare.

"Everybody stay right where you are."

Seriously? The butler did it? Who wrote this garbage? Although perhaps Hilary was supposed to be the one who actually stabbed Charles to death?

Timothy grabbed a conveniently placed motorcycle helmet from behind the bar and, alarmingly still waving his gun in our direction, began to stride cautiously over to Hilary.

"The police aren't really on their way. I never called them. And you are all to be locked inside the hotel for the night." I'm thinking this script was written before mobile phones were a thing.

And so Timothy and Hilary gathered at the front doors and we all thought the show was over until a gunshot from behind the bar was heard, banging out like a firework, followed by another one. All heads in the room turned to see Edward the bartender holding a smoking shotgun (what was with all these guns in an English manor house?). We all watched as Edward took out a police helmet and heroically placed it upon his head before the cries of Timothy and Hilary distracted us enough to turn back to them as they held their recently squeezed fake blood bags to their chests and slowly eased themselves to the floor in a rather amateurish and overly cautious way (they'd probably asked for more money to do stunt work).

Ah, right, so that would explain Edward's earlier suspicious behaviour – it was all part of the show. He probably wasn't a real actor, rather someone trained to use a weapon – ex-military, perhaps?

I suppose, after all, it was an entertaining enough night out. Quite the eye opener regarding human entertainment. I joined in the applause and howls as the cast came back in at the end and everyone was very polite about the whole shebang and I said my goodbyes to Sadie and her slumped husband who muttered something indecipherable at me as I made my exit through the same doors Timothy and Hilary had moments ago intended to make their exit through.

It was still throwing it down outside but this time I had no newspaper to cover myself. I really needed to invest in one of those umbrella things.

Hurriedly I jogged over to the small patch of woodland where I had ditched my car by the roadside and was all set to begin work on fixing the flat tyres when I noticed it was *all* the tyres that were flat. I knew I hadn't had a proper browse earlier but this was ridiculous. How could they all be flat?

I'd have to call for help with this one, as I didn't have four brand new tyres on board and so I clambered into the vehicle, relieved to be out of the rain once again and…

… not alone again.

Someone was sitting in the back seat. My third eye allows me a much better peripheral view than human eyes.

Someone with a knife — and not one covered with ketchup this time.

I see, so this wasn't simply a chance meeting. Someone had purposefully caused my tyres to pop and that same someone was now sitting in the back of my car poised to murder me and had patiently waited until this moment.

One of the orbs (or UFOs as you call them) that plague and watch your planet hovered closer to the vehicle. It knew I was in trouble. Back home, they'd be watching this stage show you know as the planet Earth with astonishment and horror.

The blade hit me too quickly to react, slashing across my neck, the knife left inside me and thrusted in further. My icky green blood sprayed liberally from the fresh wound, conversing with the splashing sounds the rain made outside on the windshield.

"Stay off our planet," were the only words the shape in the backseat aggressively uttered. He'd be one of those from the Bureau of Investigation for UFOs, I ascertained. It was too hard to tell if it was the bartender chap from the murder mystery evening, but maybe?

The blood drained from me as the orb hovered closer and pelted an impossibly bright rainbow beam of light onto the scene before it.

I heard the Bureau guy behind me fizzle into a grotesque slab of bits and pieces and gore and blood and mayhem, sending him into oblivion.

It was the last thing I saw before my own body rose toward the orb's light and I was transported far away from the distant planet Earth, full of you insects who call themselves the human race - we call you something else entirely, but I don't wish to be rude.

The knife had been absorbed into my body (I told you we can eat metal) and was utilised to shroud the once gaping wound.

Well, it certainly had been a strange journey. And, in conclusion, I probably won't go to another murder mystery night. Although I might pop along to one of those *Rocky Horror Show* audience participation screenings that I've heard about. There's no rice involved in those, right?

TRANSYLVANIAN GUESTS

Ella-Marie Wells, Tyler Owens, Stephen Perry, Greg Iatron, Kezz Hayman-Harrison, Marathon Community Theatre, Dion Watson, Aimee Dixon, Verity Smith, Lee Smith, Rosie Ludlow, Heather Ann Kaup, Sian Saunders, Leanne Clark, Tammie Glasure Anderson, Kate Hampson, Thelma Amorette Tijerina-Felton, Annette Hershfield, Lisa Barrass, Fynn Kay Kleppe, Gail Grist, Carol Fournier, Willow Usher, Mandi Usher, Kimi Loughton, Rebecca Ruth Kerry, Pat Hume (aka Gini Mini), Joann Gunby, Michael Gunby, Gordon Gunby, Lea-Ann Suthern, Antonella Quasi Giusta Panarelli, Doe Darling, David Doyon, Krysti Stern, Florence Kerr, Stan Dunse, Beth Billet, Jonna Burton, Andria Jones, Kristel Jones, David and Michele Adkinson, Adelaide & Kristen Eby, Kate Morris, Bethany Bradley, Melissa Ruth Allison, Andrina Stanislawski, Jodie Brown, Shona Walker, Alisha Davis, Angie Hatfield, Hannah Hatfield, Hayley Hatfield, Ash Reid, Lory Kramer Peacock, Boyd Goode, Steve VanMeter, Carol Barrett, Lucrezia Trezzi, Miranda Mcdonald, Richard Stegman Jr, Jaclyn Carlyle, Gemma Patricia, Todd Baker, Tracey Baker, Zoe Baker, Laigha Parry, Emily Jones, Katelyn Jones, Rosie Jones, Taylor and Emily De Meo, Heavy Petting Shadow Cast (Tucson, Arizona), Stephen Brown, Christopher McLeod, Stuart Nelson, Lucas Nelson, Aiden Nelson, Michelle Aliperto Rodriguez, Andrew Lane, Marcelle Gis, Rosalie Clarke, Samantha Clarke, Melonie DeHart, Ann Todd, Melissa Necochea, Cat Murphy, Spence Kelleway, Dee Richmond, Jared Vecchio, Annette Gillan, Jen Gauthier, Cathy Caldwell, Nathan Head, Leah Lynch, Theresa Foster, Carly Fleming, Dwight Delves, Celeste Rurehe, Robert Greene, Justin Hussey, E. Bernhard Warg, Rich Rohman, Neva Ferguson, Brooke Trotter, Gracie L Baker, Maijken Morningstar, Rachel Lara, Raven Quinn, Jessica Sheldon, Steve Storman Jr, Kaden Storman,

Sara McKee, Vicki Carrigg, Adele Webb, Teresa Koster, Rebecca Wiesniak, Desiree Lammon, Tina Lammon, Pamela Bessette, Bryan Sanderson, Paul Kramer, Robbie Drake, Francesca Angelina Scappaticcio, Keri Yates, Rob Wallis, Hayley Wilkinson, Thea Powell Jones, Kerry L Fleming, Angelia Mason, Rose Anderson, Marketta Blake, Jessica Murray, Leanne Bleakley, Emmie Whysall-Cramphorn, Katy Rose, Kieron Rose, Heatherly Dracos, Mathieu Pletcher, Hollie Ross-Watson, Angelia and Douglas Adams, Sonny Kennerley, Paula Batt, Christine Gallipeau, Rick Gallipeau, Sins of the Flesh (Players of Southern California), The Master's Servants, Monica Schneider-Ryser, Sarah Denney Jones, Kelly Jenkins, Gemma Hannigan, Natalie Warren, Kelly Warren Pritchard, Donna Potter, Lindsey Carnie, Natasha Ellis, Louise Randall, Ben Beck, Claire Hinkley, Josefine Ekroos, Jay Booth, Danielle Booth, Kyle Pettican, Liz Coultas, Lee (leemiff) Smith, Kim Cannan, Anita Pope, Deborah Drury, Katrina Storton, Melanie Grimson-Bobet, Albert Leon, Monica Schneider-Ryser, Tony Zaloudek, Tammy Ibbetson, Toni Johnson, Katie Brown, Angel Maxwell, Simon Strawford, Joan Benavidez-Sallee, Jennifer Lussier, Simon Mark Saynor, Steven Singleton, Michelle and Philip Baxter, Ann Walker-Beard, Erich Schaffer, Joanne Johnson, Jamie Jones, Michelle Hollis, Maddie CerinCeru, Nicola Donaldson Dominey, Erin Hayward, Rebecca James, Sarah Nuttall, Amber Vaughn, Jodie Taber, Casiana Isa Martinez, Ken Grant, Megan Gilby, Mikah Evans, Don McCall, Marc Forcadell Bes, Alyson Rachkoskie, Angela Vance, Paola Rossetti, Joshua and Lynzi Jermain, Jeanine Gregoire, Kate Miesnik, Jasmine Ellicott, Jae Earl (as Janet), William Woody, Jon Saunders, Angela Hernandez, Jeanna Johnston Scully, Jennifer Blasingame, Genie Blasingame, Joanna Hewitt, Kathleen WhoDat Sagers, Valerie Lion Sprinkle, Richard Sprinkle, Ruben Rivera, Emma Wojtowyez, Tina D Johnson, Lisa Taylor, Mikey Müller, Aida Dimitriou, Kelly Rickard, Katherine Hamer, Harry Hamer, Jeremy and Cara, Kalani Berry, Joe Canzoneri, Lisa

Canzoneri, Heather Brettwood, Shelia McLachlan, Gillian Green, Tracy Page, Gemma Hamon, Deona Erbacher, Lisa Levalley, Gwendolyn Berlin, Greg and Carol Gibbs, Catherine Buda, Vintie Mintie, Aston Nicholls, Devina Bailey, Patti Cash Johnson, Andrea Torrez, Tessa Mcnelly, Bethany Delacruz, Mark Munks, Andrea Pisani Adelung, Hazel Hall, Roger M Dilley, Aubia Chivers, Brian Harris, Helen Monroe McNeill, Wendy Pedretti, Marie Knight, Brad Berlin, Bekkie Williams, Scarlett Shepherd, Susan Goldsberry, Natalie Thompson, James Grouse, Jasmine Thomas, Clair Coupe, Fiona Whyte, Mel Perks, Pamela Bessette, Bryan Sanderson, Shannon Marie, Donna Carey, Sasha Bloom, Wendy Miller, Steve Miller, Jennifer Hayden, Jon Paisley, Brad Lloyd, Henri Kopecky, Sharon LoMonaco, Victoria LoMonaco, Mistress Angel, Reverend Lonni Stewart, Sarah Whyley, Mark Klasnic, Teresa Stroud, Lesley and Darren Barrows, Pamela Dickinson Donald, Shyanne Hammers, Claire and Andy Senior, Mr. Alan Scott, Rossella Chiarello, Seb Nukem, Caroline Briggs, Kelli Ktp Lis, Kevin Chagnot, Lesley Fortune, Karla May-Strange, Janice May-Strange, Pj List, Dixie Vance, Donna West, Heather Lawrence, Randy Lawrence, Sue Juffs, Jon Downs, Joyce Rosenzweig, Dani Costello, Janine McMullen, John Judge Jeffries… and Rosie Dutton, Tristan Ratterman, Jim Hetzer, Larry Viezel and The Rocky Horror Picture Show Official Fan Club in The Rocky Horror Picture Show Fan Club Group on Facebook

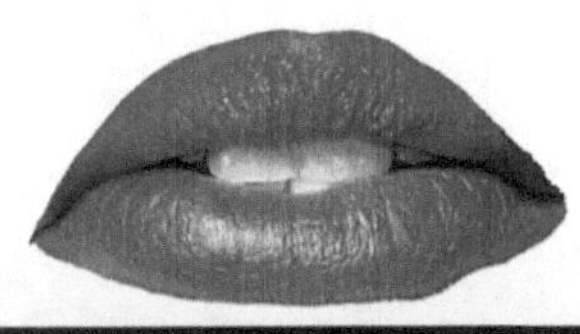
THE ROCKY
HORROR
PICTURE SHOW

THE ROCKY
HORROR
PICTURE SHOW

THE ROCKY
HORROR
PICTURE SHOW
Unauthorised
QUIZ
BOOK
WITH 200 QUESTIONS
KILLIAN H. GORE
and
PHOENIX HINKLEY

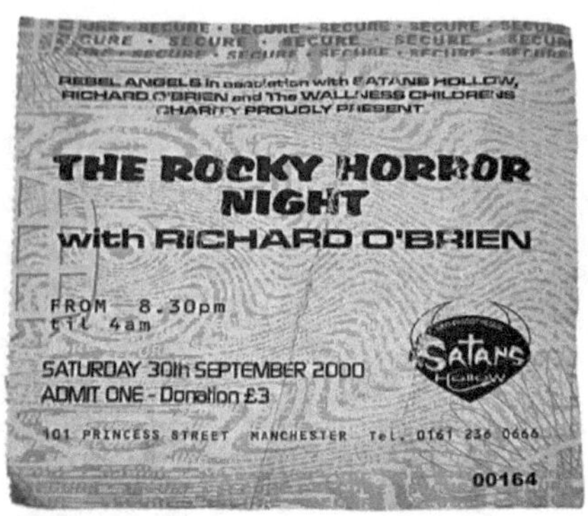

My Richard O'Brien autograph, obtained at The Rocky Horror Night at Satan's Hollow in Manchester on 30th September 2000. My cousin, Phil, and I were both incredibly drunk that night and all I can recall is we were both constantly patting Richard O'Brien's head! Apologies to Mr. O'Brien if he is still traumatised by that strange night out. In fact, we were so drunk that my cousin awoke the next morning and realised he'd unwittingly obtained two autographs from Richard O'Brien!

My programme and ticket from seeing The Rocky Horror Show on the 27th of November 1991 at the Liverpool Empire – on a school trip. Peter Blake was Frank-N-Furter. The rest of the cast were: Zalie Burrow as Janet, Kate O'Sullivan as Magenta, Paul Reeves as Brad, Peter Bayliss as The Narrator, Stuart Bennett as Riff Raff, Mark Heenehan as Eddie/Dr Scott, Julia Hampson as Columbia and Adam Caine as Rocky